THE ORDER OF MELCHIZEDEK

THE ETERNAL PRIESTHOOD OF CHRIST REVEALED

UNVEILING THE MYSTERY HIDDEN FROM AGES -
FROM ABRAHAM TO THE THRONE OF HEAVEN

DAMIANO B. CENTOLA

EXPLORA BOOKS
700 – 838 West Hastings St. Vancouver
BC V6C 0A6
www.explorabooks.com
Phone: (604) 330 6795

No part of this book may be reproduced, stored in a retrieval system, or transmitted by any means without the written permission of the author.

Because of the dynamic nature of the Internet, any web addresses or links contained in this book may have changed since publication and may no longer be valid. The views expressed in this work are solely those of the author and do not necessarily reflect the views of the publisher, and the publisher hereby disclaims any responsibility for them.

Bible verses are quoted from the King James Version (KJV), which is public domain, the English Standard Version (ESV), and the New King James Version (NKJV).

ISBN: 978-1-83430-063-4 *(Paperback)*
978-1-83430-064-1 *(Hardback)*
978-1-83430-065-8 *(eBook)*

© 2025 Damiano B. Centola. All rights reserved.

THE ORDER OF MELCHIZEDEK

Table of Contents

Preface i

Introduction iii

Chapter I
The Appearance in the Valley — Bread, Wine, and Blessing 1

Chapter II
A Priest Without Beginning — The Mystery of No Lineage 5

Chapter III
King of Righteousness, King of Peace — The Double Crown 9

Chapter IV
The Tithe of Abraham — Acknowledging the Greater 15

Chapter V
Psalm 110 — A Thunderclap from Eternity 21

Chapter VI
The Levitical Priesthood Fades — A Superior Order Rises 25

Chapter VII
The Priest Who Lives Forever — Yeshua and Melchizedek Unified 31

Chapter VIII
The Heavenly Sanctuary — Priesthood Beyond the Veil 39

Chapter IX
The End of the Old, The Reign of the Eternal 49

Conclusion 53

Glossary of Terms 55

Scripture Index 57

Bibliography & References 61

Acknowledgments 65

About the Author 67

Back Cover Blurb 69

Preface

There is a name hidden in Scripture like a flame behind the veil—a name that appears briefly, enigmatically, and then echoes across the corridors of redemptive history: Melchizedek.

Who is he? Why does his story, spanning only a few verses in Genesis, reverberate with such intensity through the Psalms and thunder again in the Book of Hebrews? What mystery did Abraham bow before? What eternal reality did David glimpse in the Spirit? And what royal priesthood now stands open to the redeemed, not by the blood of bulls, but by the blood of the Lamb?

This book was born from awe. Not merely curiosity—but reverent trembling before the majesty of a revelation that pierces time. The figure of Melchizedek is not a puzzle for scholars only—it is a blazing key to understanding the identity and eternal role of our Lord, Yeshua the Messiah. He is not only King of Kings—He is also High Priest forever after the order of Melchizedek. This order is not earthly. It is not inherited through flesh. It is heavenly. Eternal. Perfect.

And it is calling us.

In an age of confusion, spiritual compromise, and religious division, the Spirit is lifting our eyes to something ancient, pure, and indestructible—a priesthood not based on man's merit, but God's majesty. It is a priesthood that cannot be shaken. One that spans from

Salem to Zion, from the valley where Abram tithed to the throne where the Lamb intercedes.

This book is a journey into that mystery.

We will walk through the sacred intersections of Scripture—from the tented plains of Genesis to the unshakable kingdom revealed in Hebrews.

We will bow with Abraham. We will listen to David's prophetic thunder. We will step into the heavenly tabernacle with the risen Messiah, and we will discover, by grace, that this priesthood is not only about Him—but about us. A royal priesthood. A holy nation. A people made new.

To all who long for deeper worship, stronger identity, and clearer access to the throne of God—this is your heritage. This is your inheritance.

This is the Order of Melchizedek.

— Damiano B. Centola

Introduction

Unveiling a Forgotten Order — From Shadows to Substance

In the grand drama of redemption, there are names that dominate the stage—Abraham, Moses, David, Paul. But tucked quietly between the lines, there are names that burn like coals beneath the surface—mysterious, eternal, bursting with untapped revelation.

Melchizedek is one of those names.

He appears for a moment in Genesis 14—no origin, no ending—bearing bread and wine, blessing Abram in the name of God "Most High." Then he vanishes into silence. No genealogy. No tomb. No recorded lineage. Just the echo of a blessing and the shadow of something far greater.

And then, a thousand years later, David hears it again—this time from heaven:

> *"The Lord hath sworn, and will not repent, Thou art a priest for ever after the order of Melchizedek." (Psalm 110:4, KJV)*

Another thousand years pass. And suddenly, the veil is torn.

A crucified Messiah rises. And the writer of Hebrews declares what few had understood for millennia:

This Melchizedek is the key.

Not just a type. Not just a symbol. But a witness to an eternal priesthood, outside the laws of Levi. A divine order that preceded Moses, fulfilled David's vision, and is now embodied forever in Jesus the Messiah.

This is not theological novelty. This is divine architecture.

The Order of Melchizedek is not an Old Testament relic—it is the spiritual reality that defines our salvation today. It tells us not only who Jesus is, but what He is doing right now in the heavens. And just as importantly, it shows us who we are becoming as His redeemed—priests in His likeness, royal servants in a kingdom not built by hands.

This book is written not for the curious only—but for the called.

For those who sense there is more behind the curtain.

For those who long to go beyond Sunday religion and enter into the living priesthood of Christ.

For those who want to burn—not just believe.

You are not just saved. You are being consecrated.

You are not just forgiven. You are being fitted for an order that existed before time and shall never end.

This is not merely theology. This is destiny.

Welcome to the mystery.
Welcome to the fire.
Welcome to The Order of Melchizedek.

— Damiano B. Centola

Chapter I
The Appearance in the Valley — Bread, Wine, and Blessing

Genesis 14:18–20

In the dry windswept valley of Shaveh, after a battle that could have altered the course of history, a mysterious figure steps into the narrative of Scripture like lightning in the dark— brilliant, brief, and unforgettable. His name is Melchizedek.

There are no horns or chariots. No prophecy or forewarning. He simply appears.

"And Melchizedek king of Salem brought forth bread and wine: and he was the priest of the most high God. And he blessed him, and said, Blessed be Abram of the most high God, possessor of heaven and earth: And blessed be the most high God, which hath delivered thine enemies into thy hand. And he gave him tithes of all."

(Genesis 14:18–20, KJV)

The moment is easy to overlook—a three-verse encounter between two men. But hidden within this exchange is a revelation that stretches from Eden to Eternity. It is here that the priesthood of Christ is first glimpsed. It is here that heaven acknowledges earth, and earth responds in worship. It is here that the priesthood not of man, but of God, is unveiled.

A Priest Appears — Without Origin, Without End

At this point in the Genesis narrative, Abram has just rescued his nephew Lot from a coalition of kings. He has refused the spoils of war from the King of Sodom. He is weary but victorious. And then, without introduction, Melchizedek comes—bearing bread and wine.

We are told three things about him:

1. He is king of Salem.
2. He is priest of the Most High God (El Elyon).
3. He brings bread and wine and blesses Abram.

Each of these details is theologically explosive. And each will later be fulfilled—and surpassed—in Christ.

The name Melchizedek means "King of Righteousness". The place he reigns—Salem—is often associated with Jerusalem, and the word means "peace." He is therefore King of Righteousness and King of Peace—a dual identity not shared by any other priest or king in the Old Testament. But this is no ordinary man.

Bread and Wine — A Foretaste of a Greater Covenant

Before law, before sacrifice, before Levitical rituals—this priest of the Most High offers bread and wine.

Why not blood and fire? Why not lambs and smoke?

Because this moment is not about ritual. It is about covenant. And what Melchizedek brings is not just refreshment for Abram's body—it is a symbolic precursor of the Lord's Supper, the broken bread and poured-out wine of the Messiah to come.

It is as if heaven was already whispering, long before Calvary, "This is My body... This is My blood..."

Abram receives it. He accepts the offering. And he responds not just with gratitude—but with worship.

He gives Melchizedek a tithe of all—a full tenth of the spoils. Not because Melchizedek demanded it, but because Abram recognized the greater. The writer of Hebrews confirms this:

> *"And without all contradiction the less is blessed of the better."*
> *(Hebrews 7:7)*

This act is stunning. Abram—the father of nations, the one who would become Abraham—bows in spirit to a priest whose order is older than Levi, higher than Aaron, and eternal in scope.

A Shadow of Things to Come

What makes this encounter so profound is its brevity and weight.

Melchizedek has no recorded ancestry, no backstory, no death. He simply arrives, ministers, and fades.

But Scripture never forgets.

David would later write in Psalm 110:

> *"The Lord hath sworn, and will not repent, Thou art a priest for ever after the order of Melchizedek."*

And Hebrews will cry out:

> *"This Melchizedek... abideth a priest continually." (Hebrews 7:3)*

This was not just a man—it was a manifestation of an eternal order.

What It Means for Us

The meeting in the valley is not just history. It is prophetic design. It tells us:

- That the priesthood of Christ is not an invention of the New Testament, but a fulfillment of something ancient.
- That our access to God is not through Levi, but through the Bread and the Wine—through Christ.
- That blessing flows from heaven's priest, and worship flows upward in response.

It also reminds us that true spiritual authority is often quiet, humble, and sudden. It does not always announce itself with grandeur. Sometimes it appears, ministers, and departs—leaving behind the fragrance of eternity.

You and I are the children of Abraham by faith. The same bread. The same wine. The same blessing.

So let us bow, as Abram did—not to a man, but to the King of Righteousness.

Chapter II
A Priest Without Beginning – The Mystery of No Lineage

"Without father, without mother, without descent, having neither beginning of days, nor end of life; but made like unto the Son of God; abideth a priest continually."

(Hebrews 7:3)

There are mysteries in Scripture that echo like thunder from a distant place. They shake the foundations of theology and compel us to fall silent before their depth. One of the greatest of these is the statement above—about a priest with no genealogy.
In a Bible filled with lineages, why does Melchizedek's silence scream so loud?
In the ancient Hebrew world, lineage was everything. Authority—especially priestly authority—was inherited. Aaron's sons became priests. The Levites served because of their tribe. Every name was connected to a father, a grandfather, a house, a legacy. If you had no pedigree, you had no position.

But suddenly, in Genesis 14, here comes Melchizedek—without father, without mother, without descent.

This is not to say he was never born, or that he was some angelic being. What the Scriptures emphasize is this: his priesthood is not tied to human lineage. His credentials do not come from his ancestry. His authority does not descend from man, but from heaven itself.

No Beginning, No End — A Type Beyond Time

The writer of Hebrews makes the case: Melchizedek is a type—a living preview—of Christ. He is not the Son of God, but is "made like unto" the Son. The comparison is intentional.

The Messiah would not be a Levite.

He would not inherit a priesthood through Moses.

He would rise outside the system—and yet fulfill it perfectly.

Melchizedek's priesthood is timeless. It has no recorded beginning, no ending. And in this, we see the shadow of the one who is Alpha and Omega, the priest who ever lives to make intercession.

Yeshua did not become a priest because of ancestral rights, but because of divine appointment:

"Thou art a priest forever, after the order of Melchizedek." (Psalm 110:4)

This means that His priesthood is not temporal, like that of Aaron. It is eternal. And what does that mean for us?

It means our salvation is not fragile. It is anchored in a priest who never dies, whose ministry never ends, whose authority never lapses. There is no succession plan because there is no need for one.

The Silence That Speaks

It is easy to overlook the significance of what the Bible leaves unsaid. But in Melchizedek's case, the absence of genealogy is not an oversight—it is the very point.

His story is left open, suspended in mystery, because he is not the focus. He is a signpost. A foreshadow. A figure meant to prepare the stage for the arrival of someone greater.

Hebrews does not idolize Melchizedek. It reveals that he was a type—a mirror reflection—meant to help us recognize the real priest, who has now come:

> *"For it is evident that our Lord sprang out of Judah; of which tribe Moses spake nothing concerning priesthood." (Hebrews 7:14)*

So if Jesus is not of Levi, how can He be our priest?

Because His priesthood is not human—it is heavenly.

Why This Matters Now

In today's world, identity is often tied to background—name, race, credentials, bloodline, ancestry kits. People want to know where they came from, because it helps define who they are.

But Melchizedek is a disruption to that thinking.

He shows us a priesthood that is not from below, but from above. And in Christ, you and I are invited into something just as radical:

> *"Ye are a chosen generation, a royal priesthood, an holy nation, a peculiar people..." (1 Peter 2:9)*

Not by birth.

Not by merit.

Not by ancestry.

But by divine election.

This mystery of Melchizedek tells us: God is not bound by man's systems. He raises up His priest on His terms. And that priest now sits at His right hand, forever interceding for us.

You are not saved because you come from the right stock.

You are saved because your priest has no end.

And because He lives forever, you will too.

Chapter III
King of Righteousness, King of Peace — The Double Crown

"To whom also Abraham gave a tenth part of all; first being by interpretation King of Righteousness, and after that also King of Salem, which is, King of Peace."
— *Hebrews 7:2*

In ancient times, names were not just labels — they were identities, often prophetic. A name could speak of a person's mission, their role, or their nature. This is especially true in Scripture, where names are often packed with divine insight.

And in the case of Melchizedek, we are given two names — two thrones, as it were — and both are astonishing.

He is called:
- Melek-Tzedek — "King of Righteousness"
- Melek-Shalem (Salem) — "King of Peace"

These are not empty titles. They are a theological key, unlocking a portrait of Christ before Bethlehem.

The Crown of Righteousness

"Melchizedek" literally means "king of righteousness." This is not merely moral decency. In Hebrew thought, tzedek refers to divine justice, rightness in the eyes of God, and covenant faithfulness. This kind of righteousness flows from God Himself.

To say that someone is "king of righteousness" is to say that they govern by the standard of heaven.

The Levitical priests offered sacrifices for sin, because the people (and they themselves) were unrighteous. But Melchizedek stands apart — there is no sacrifice mentioned in Genesis 14. No blood of bulls or goats. Instead, he comes out with bread and wine — the symbols of fellowship and covenant.

He is not merely managing sin. He is ushering in a higher kind of kingdom — one where righteousness reigns and communion is restored.

This is exactly the kind of reign the Messiah would bring:

> *"Behold, a king shall reign in righteousness..." (Isaiah 32:1)*
>
> *"...the Lord our Righteousness." (Jeremiah 23:6)*

Yeshua is not just righteous — He is our righteousness. In Him, we become what we could never achieve on our own. Melchizedek, the king of righteousness, points forward to the One who would fulfill that name with flesh and blood.

The Crown of Peace

But Melchizedek is not just king of righteousness. He is also king of Salem — a place that would later be called Jeru-Salem.

Salem means peace — not just the absence of war, but shalom: completeness, wholeness, harmony with God.

The order is important. First comes righteousness, then comes peace.

> *"And the work of righteousness shall be peace..." (Isaiah 32:17)*

There can be no true peace without righteousness. There can be no wholeness if we are still fractured by sin.

Yeshua, the true Melchizedek, comes as both:
- The righteous judge, who fulfills the law and bears its penalty.
- The prince of peace, who reconciles God and man through His blood.

"Therefore being justified by faith, we have peace with God through our Lord Jesus Christ..." (Romans 5:1)

This is not symbolic poetry. This is a heavenly reality.

The Two Crowns Become One

In ancient Israel, kings came from the line of Judah. Priests came from the line of Levi. The two roles were separate by law. Any attempt to merge them was met with severe consequences (see King Uzziah, 2 Chronicles 26).

But Melchizedek is both king and priest.

And so is Yeshua.

He wears both crowns:
- A priestly crown, because He mediates between God and man.
- A royal crown, because He rules with all authority in heaven and earth.

This double crown is what the prophet Zechariah foresaw when he said:

"He shall be a priest upon His throne..." (Zechariah 6:13)

In Messiah, righteousness and peace are not two separate roads. They meet — and kiss:

"Mercy and truth are met together; righteousness and peace have kissed each other." (Psalm 85:10)

This is the divine harmony of the Melchizedek order.

What This Means for Us

You and I live in a world of broken peace and corrupted justice. Kings rule by power, not righteousness. Peace is negotiated, not born of truth.

But in Yeshua, the true Melchizedek, we are brought under a better crown.

He makes us righteous by His blood.

He gives us peace through His Spirit.

And He invites us to share in His reign:

> *"They shall be priests of God and of Christ, and shall reign with Him a thousand years." (Revelation 20:6)*

The order of Melchizedek is not only about the past — it is a present reality and a future promise. We serve the One who wears the double crown.

Not just a Savior.

Not just a King.

But a Priest-King.

He is righteousness. He is peace and his name is Yeshua.

Chapter IV
The Tithe of Abraham — Acknowledging the Greater

> *"Now consider how great this man was, unto whom even the patriarch Abraham gave the tenth of the spoils."*
>
> *— Hebrews 7:4*

In the wake of a great battle, Abraham emerged victorious. He had risked everything to rescue his nephew Lot from the coalition of kings. Blood had been shed. Spoils had been seized. The warrior-patriarch stood triumphant. And yet, as he returned from battle, he did something radical — something unprecedented.

He bowed.

Not before a king of Sodom. Not before his allies. But before a man cloaked in mystery and majesty — Melchizedek, the priest of the Most High God.

And he gave him a tenth of everything.

The Tithe Before the Law

This is the first time in Scripture the concept of tithing is mentioned. And it appears not in the Law of Moses, but centuries earlier — in the days of Abram, long before Sinai.

This is not legal obligation.

It is not ritual.

It is reverence.

Abraham's tithe was a spontaneous act of honor. He was recognizing something that transcended bloodlines and tribes: authority from heaven. He saw in Melchizedek a priest not made by man, but by divine appointment.

By giving a tenth, Abraham declared:

"This one is greater than I."

It is no small thing. Abraham is the patriarch — the chosen vessel of God, the father of the faith, the one through whom nations would be blessed.

And yet, he gives. He bows. He yields.

Why the Tenth?

The number ten in Scripture symbolizes completeness in human responsibility:

- Ten commandments.
- Ten plagues in Egypt.
- Ten virgins in the parable of Jesus.

A tithe — a tenth — represents the whole being submitted.

When Abraham gave a tenth of the spoils, it was not just about generosity. It was a statement: "All that I have belongs to God. And this priest, Melchizedek, stands as the appointed steward of that divine transaction."

This moment echoed far beyond the valley of Shaveh. It set in motion a pattern of worship and acknowledgment that the Levitical priesthood would later imitate — and that the New Testament would later surpass.

A Greater Priesthood Acknowledged

The book of Hebrews reflects deeply on this moment:

"And without all contradiction the less is blessed of the better."
(Hebrews 7:7)

In Jewish culture, the greater always blesses the lesser. The fact that Melchizedek blesses Abraham — and Abraham receives it — is a theological earthquake.

Abraham, in a sense, represents all his descendants — even Levi, the tribe of priests yet unborn. Hebrews tells us that Levi paid tithes through Abraham:

"For he was yet in the loins of his father, when Melchizedek met him."

(Hebrews 7:10)

In other words, the entire Levitical priesthood bowed in Abraham.

This is no minor moment. It is a divine declaration:

A greater priesthood has arrived.

One not based on ancestry, but on eternity.

One that will not fade or fail.

Yeshua and the Better Offering

Now consider Yeshua, who came in the order of Melchizedek.

He did not offer bulls or goats.

He did not minister in the temple of Jerusalem.

He offered Himself — the perfect tithe, the firstfruit of resurrection, the complete surrender of heaven's treasure.

"For by one offering he hath perfected forever them that are sanctified." (Hebrews 10:14)

If Abraham gave a tenth of the spoils of war, Yeshua gave the fullness of Himself after the war of the cross.

What Abraham did symbolically in a valley, Christ did cosmically on Calvary.

And we, like Abraham, are invited to respond.

What This Means for Us

We are children of Abraham, not just by genealogy, but by faith. And like Abraham, we are called to:

- Recognize the greater
- Honor the eternal
- Respond with surrender

The Melchizedek priesthood calls us out of mechanical religion and into relational reverence. It invites us to offer our first, not our leftovers — our hearts, not just our hands.

Tithing is not a tax.

It is an act of alignment.

It says, "I trust the One who reigns in righteousness and peace. I honor the One who reigns from heaven."

It is not about numbers.

It is about kneeling.

And when we kneel to this Priest-King — the true Melchizedek, Yeshua the Christ — we are blessed in return, just as Abraham was:

> *"Blessed be Abram of the most high God, possessor of heaven and earth..." (Genesis 14:19)*

Psalm 110 – A Thunderclap from Eternity

Chapter V
Psalm 110
– A Thunderclap from Eternity

"The Lord hath sworn, and will not repent, Thou art a priest for ever after the order of Melchizedek."

— Psalm 110:4

Psalm 110 stands like a thunderclap in the heavens—brief, jolting, and eternal in its echo. Of all the Psalms, this is the one most frequently quoted in the New Testament. It is Davidic, messianic, and prophetic. It is God-breathed poetry embedded with heavenly decrees. The fourth verse, in particular, is one of the most significant divine pronouncements in all of Scripture: "The Lord hath sworn, and will not repent, Thou art a priest for ever after the order of Melchizedek."

It is as though God, who rarely swears with an oath, opens His mouth in this Psalm to declare something irrevocable. The eternal priesthood of the Messiah is not a quiet teaching, hidden in a shadow—it is a decree from the very throne of God. And with that decree, the figure of Melchizedek, long silent since Genesis 14, suddenly roars back into Scripture after a thousand years.

A Psalm of the Future Spoken in the Past

The setting of Psalm 110 is crucial. Written by David, it reveals truths that he himself could never fully comprehend apart from divine revelation. The Psalm begins with "The LORD said unto my Lord, Sit thou at my right hand, until I make thine enemies thy footstool." This is not David speaking of himself; it is Yahweh speaking to Adonai—the Father to the Son, the Ancient of Days to the Eternal One.

This establishes Psalm 110 as a Messianic Psalm par excellence. Jesus Himself quoted this Psalm to confound the Pharisees in Matthew 22, asking, "If David then call him Lord, how is he his son?" In that one question, Jesus pointed directly to His divinity, preexistence, and kingly authority—grounded in Psalm 110.

But the king in this psalm is also a priest, and not just any priest. He is not of Levi. He is not of Aaron. He is of Melchizedek.

Sworn by God: The Gravity of Divine Oath

The language is striking: "The LORD hath sworn, and will not repent." God's swearing is rare in Scripture. He swore by Himself to Abraham. He swore by His holiness in Psalm 89. And here, He swears that the coming Messiah will be a priest forever—not temporarily, not conditionally, not until death—but forever.

This irrevocable oath is foundational. It means the priesthood of Melchizedek is eternal, superior, and divinely appointed. The Levitical priesthood had succession and death. The Melchizedekian priesthood has no beginning, no end, and no earthly genealogy. It is not subject to time, temple, or tribe. It is rooted in the eternal counsel of God.

In Hebrews 7:21, this verse is quoted again to show the superiority of Christ's priesthood over the Levitical order. The writer of Hebrews calls attention to the permanence and perfection of Jesus' priestly work, grounded not in law, but in oath.

A King-Priest: The Reunification of Roles

Psalm 110 restores something that had been separated in Israel's history: the roles of king and priest. Under Mosaic law, the king could not serve as priest, and the priest could not be king. Saul was judged for overstepping that boundary. Uzziah was struck with leprosy for trying to burn incense in the temple.

But in Melchizedek, the two roles are combined. He was both king of Salem and priest of the Most High God. And in Psalm 110, the Messiah is declared both king and priest forever.

This is profound. It means that the One who rules also intercedes. The One who bears the scepter also bears the incense. The One seated on the throne is the same One who ministers at the altar.

This dual office finds perfect fulfillment in Yeshua, who is both our righteous King and our great High Priest. He wears the crown and the ephod. He governs and redeems. He rules and reconciles. He reigns in righteousness and pleads in mercy. No other figure in Scripture holds this dual role in such perfect harmony.

Forever — The Word that Changes Everything

The key word in Psalm 110:4 is "forever." It is the Hebrew word olam, meaning eternal, everlasting, without end. It means that the priesthood inaugurated by Melchizedek and fulfilled in Christ is not a temporary bridge—it is the eternal highway between God and man.

In the Levitical order, priests grew old and died. Sacrifices were repeated. The altar was never cold. But in the order of Melchizedek, there is no decay, no succession, no fading away. One Priest. One offering. One intercession. Forever.

Hebrews 7:24–25 puts it this way: "But this man, because he continueth ever, hath an unchangeable priesthood. Wherefore he is able also to save them to the uttermost that come unto God by him, seeing he ever liveth to make intercession for them."

This is the priesthood that saves to the uttermost—not partially, not temporarily, but completely and eternally.

A Thunderclap Across the Ages

Psalm 110 was written over a millennium before Christ walked the earth. Yet it echoed through the generations, rippling through prophets, scribes, and sages. It was whispered in temple courts, memorized by faithful Jews, and awaited with messianic longing.

Then one day, in the fullness of time, the Word became flesh. And the eternal priest stepped into time—not through the line of Levi, but through the decree of Psalm 110.

This Psalm thundered at His baptism, "This is my beloved Son." It roared at the cross when the veil was torn. It echoed at the resurrection when the tomb was empty. And it resounds even now in the heavens where He intercedes for His people—not as a Levite, but as the priest forever after the order of Melchizedek.

The Psalm That Seals the Priesthood

Psalm 110 is not just a poetic declaration. It is a covenantal seal. It is the Father's pronouncement over the Son. It is the legal grounding of Christ's priestly ministry in heaven and His salvific power on earth.

This Psalm does what no Levitical ritual ever could—it anchors our hope in the eternally unchanging High Priest who sits at the right hand of the Father. In Him, the order of Melchizedek is not a shadow—it is a living reality. He is our King. He is our Priest. He is our everlasting Hope.

Chapter VI
The Levitical Priesthood Fades — A Superior Order Rises

"For the priesthood being changed, there is made of necessity a change also of the law."
— Hebrews 7:12

The tabernacle once stood in the wilderness, glowing with gold and echoing with the bleating of sacrificial animals. Priests in linen garments carried out sacred duties—offering incense, sprinkling blood, tending the lampstand. The tribe of Levi was chosen to stand before God and minister daily. They were the mediators, the intercessors, the ordained.

But the Levitical priesthood, though instituted by God, was never meant to be permanent. It served its purpose as a tutor, a shadow, a foreshadowing of something far greater. And when the reality came, the shadow began to fade.

In this chapter, we turn to the letter to the Hebrews—a masterpiece of theological clarity—where the apostolic writer systematically unveils the transition from the temporary priesthood of Levi to the eternal priesthood of Melchizedek, fulfilled in Yeshua the Messiah.

The Limitations of Levi

The Levitical priesthood was bound by bloodline, ceremony, geography, and mortality. A man could not volunteer for the office—he had to be born into it, descended from Aaron. The law prescribed every detail of priestly life, from garments to grain offerings, from consecration rituals to death rites.

But Hebrews 7–10 lays bare its weaknesses:

- It could not make anyone perfect. (*Hebrews 7:11*)
- Its priests were mortal and subject to sin. (*Hebrews 7:23, 27*)
- Its sacrifices were continual and incomplete. (*Hebrews 10:1-4*)
- Its sanctuary was made with hands—a copy of the heavenly. (*Hebrews 9:24*)

These were not flaws, but built-in limitations. The Levitical system was never meant to be the final word—it was meant to prepare hearts for something greater.

A Priest Arises from Another Tribe

Hebrews 7:13–14 makes an astonishing point: Jesus, our High Priest, came from the tribe of Judah, a tribe about which nothing was ever said concerning priesthood.

> *"For he of whom these things are spoken pertaineth to another tribe, of which no man gave attendance at the altar."*

This statement is revolutionary. It means the priesthood was no longer about tribe or birthright. God was doing something completely new—a priest not from Aaron, but from Melchizedek; not from Sinai, but from Zion; not from the law of a carnal commandment, but from the power of an endless life.

The Change of the Law

Hebrews 7:12 is one of the most seismic theological statements in the New Testament:

> *"For the priesthood being changed, there is made of necessity a change also of the law."*

The Levitical priesthood and the Mosaic Law were joined together like body and shadow. If one changed, so must the other. The arrival of a new, eternal Priest signals the dawn of a new covenant—written not on stone tablets, but on hearts.

This doesn't mean God's righteousness changed. Rather, the means by which access to God is granted has shifted—from repeated sacrifices by mortal priests to one eternal offering by the immortal Son.

A Better Hope Is Introduced

Hebrews 7:19:

> *"For the law made nothing perfect, but the bringing in of a better hope did; by the which we draw nigh unto God."*

The phrase "a better hope" is the heartbeat of this new priesthood. The Levitical order created distance—curtains, rituals, washings, exclusions. But through Melchizedek's line, and through Yeshua's finished work, the veil is torn. We now draw near to God—not by ritual, but by relationship; not by blood of bulls, but by the blood of the Lamb.

The superiority of the Melchizedek order is not just theoretical—it is deeply personal. You and I now have access to the holy of holies—not once a year, but every moment. This is the better hope.

The Oath That Establishes Permanence

Unlike Aaron's priesthood, which was established by law and genealogy, Jesus 'priesthood was established by an oath from God Himself:

> *"The Lord sware and will not repent, Thou art a priest forever after the order of Melchizedek." (Psalm 110:4, quoted in Hebrews 7:21)*

This oath establishes Christ's priesthood as eternal, unchangeable, and supreme. It cannot be repealed, replaced, or retired. It is the priesthood that stands even now in the heavenly sanctuary, where Christ ministers at the right hand of the Father.

Unchangeable, Eternal, and Personal
Hebrews 7:24–25:

> *"But this man, because he continueth ever, hath an unchangeable priesthood. Wherefore he is able also to save them to the uttermost that come unto God by him, seeing he ever liveth to make intercession for them."*

This is the heartbeat of the gospel. Jesus, as our eternal priest, is not merely a symbol or shadow—He is the active intercessor, praying for us, defending us, covering us.

- "Unchangeable" (Greek: aparabatos) means permanent, inviolable, nontransferable.
- "Ever liveth" reminds us that His resurrection was not just victory over death—it was the foundation of His priesthood.
- "Save to the uttermost" means there is no limit to His reach—He saves completely, eternally, and without fail.

The Curtain Falls — And Rises Again
When Yeshua died on the cross, the curtain in the temple was torn in two—from top to bottom. This was not symbolic destruction; it was divine transition. The earthly priesthood was finished. The heavenly priesthood had begun.

The Levitical order faded like the setting sun, and the order of Melchizedek rose like the dawn. What was once carried out in shadows and ceremonies is now fulfilled in spirit and truth.

Worship in Spirit and Truth
The new priesthood also redefines worship. We no longer come to earthly temples with goats and incense—we come through Jesus, the living Way.

We lift our hands not in fear of being unclean, but in boldness before the throne of grace.

This priesthood is not passive theology. It shapes everything:

- How we pray — with bold access
- How we live — in righteousness and peace
- How we worship — with unveiled faces
- How we suffer — knowing our High Priest sympathizes with us
- How we hope — anchored in a priest who never dies

The Fading Shadow and the Rising Light

The Levitical priesthood had its place, but it was a placeholder. It was a tent, not a temple; a type, not the truth; a preparation, not the fulfillment. Now that the true High Priest has come, we are no longer under the old shadows. We are under grace, truth, and an eternal intercession that cannot be broken.

The priesthood has changed. The altar has changed. The law has changed. And because of that, our access has changed.

Forever.

Chapter VII
The Priest Who Lives Forever — Yeshua and Melchizedek Unified

"But this man, because he continueth ever, hath an unchangeable priesthood."
— Hebrews 7:24

We now stand at the highest peak of this mystery—Melchizedek not merely as a prophetic figure, but as the shadow of the Son who was to come. Yeshua, the Messiah, is not only in the order of Melchizedek—He is the embodiment of that eternal priesthood. This is not typology alone—it is fulfillment in radiant glory.

The name Melchizedek means King of Righteousness, and he was also King of Salem, which means Peace. These are not random titles. They are the very essence of who Christ is: our righteousness and our peace. *(Jeremiah 23:6; Ephesians 2:14)*

"This Man…"

Hebrews 7:24 begins, "But this man…"

The phrase is thunderous in context. After recounting the mortality of the Levitical priests—who were many because they died—this declaration comes like a trumpet:

This man—Jesus—continues forever.

This man has an unchangeable priesthood.

This man is able to save to the uttermost.

We are not dealing with metaphor. We are dealing with the living Son of God, who stepped into time, fulfilled prophecy, died once, rose eternally, and now stands—bodily—in heaven as our Great High Priest.

The Priest Who Is Also the Sacrifice

No Levitical priest ever offered himself. They brought bulls, lambs, and goats. But Yeshua, as both Priest and Lamb, offered Himself.

Hebrews 9:12 says:

"Neither by the blood of goats and calves, but by his own blood he entered in once into the holy place, having obtained eternal redemption for us."

This is the mystery of Melchizedek taken to its full cosmic conclusion:

- Not only a priest,
- Not only a king,
- But the very offering, altar, and doorway.

Eternal Intercession

What is Jesus doing now? He is not resting from His redemptive labor. He is interceding.

Hebrews 7:25:

"Wherefore he is able also to save them to the uttermost that come unto God by him, seeing he ever liveth to make intercession for them."

This is not poetic flourish. It is the present-tense reality of heaven's throne room. Right now, Jesus is speaking over you. Praying over you. Advocating for you.

His priesthood is not limited to Calvary—it extends into the heavenlies, where He speaks mercy over the accused and whispers strength into the weary.

A Better Covenant, A Better Priest

Hebrews 8:6 says:

> *"But now hath he obtained a more excellent ministry, by how much also he is the mediator of a better covenant, which was established upon better promises."*

This covenant—ratified by His blood—is not etched on stone tablets but on human hearts. And this priesthood—rooted in the heavens—is not subject to aging, corruption, or succession.

He will never die. He will never retire. He will never need a replacement. This is the priesthood that cannot fail.

Beyond the Veil

When Yeshua ascended, He passed through the heavens (*Hebrews 4:14*). He entered not into a manmade sanctuary, but into the heavenly holy of holies (*Hebrews 9:24*).

Why? Because Melchizedek's priesthood always pointed above.

- Above Levi.
- Above law.
- Above earthly tabernacles.
- Above ritual and regulation.
- Above sin and death.

We now have a heavenly priest, seated at the right hand of God, who still ministers. Not with animal blood, but with His own. Not with trembling, but with triumph. Not with temporary results, but eternal ones.

The One Mediator

1 Timothy 2:5 declares:

> *"For there is one God, and one mediator between God and men, the man Christ Jesus."*

Melchizedek reminds us: there is only One.

Not Mary. Not saints. Not popes. Not pastors.

Only Jesus can bring us to the Father.

This is the scandal and the glory of the gospel. Access to God is no longer regulated by human offices—but by divine blood. Not by the Temple in Jerusalem—but by the Temple in Heaven.

The Fulfillment, Not Just the Foreshadow

Many see Melchizedek only as a type. But the Scriptures declare that Yeshua is after the order of Melchizedek—not a new invention, but the eternal pattern.

- He is the true King of Righteousness.
- He is the true King of Peace.
- He brings out bread and wine—the symbols of His body and blood.
- He blesses the children of Abraham—and becomes their promise fulfilled.

This is not mythology. This is majesty.

And it is the glory of Jesus Christ.

The Priest Who Sits
Hebrews 10:12:

> *"But this man, after he had offered one sacrifice for sins forever, sat down on the right hand of God."*

In the earthly temple, the priests never sat. There were no chairs in the Holy Place. Why? Because their work was never done. Sin kept coming. Blood kept flowing.

But this Priest—this Melchizedekian Messiah—sat down. His work was finished. His intercession continues, but His sacrifice was once and for all. He sat—because it is done.

From Salem to the Skies

Melchizedek was king of Salem—which would become Jerusalem.
But Yeshua is the High Priest of Heavenly Jerusalem, the city whose builder and maker is God (*Hebrews 11:10*).

We are no longer anchored to an earthly temple. We are drawn into a heavenly Zion, where the Lamb is the light, and where the throne of grace is open to all who believe.

Conclusion: One Priest, Forever

There is only one priest who can carry your name into the presence of God.

There is only one who wears the breastplate with your name written on His heart.

There is only one who offered blood that cannot decay.

There is only one who lives to intercede for you.

There is only one whose priesthood is eternal.

His name is Yeshua.

He is after the order of Melchizedek.

And He will never let you go.

Chapter VIII
The Heavenly Sanctuary — Priesthood Beyond the Veil

> *"For Christ is not entered into the holy places made with hands... but into heaven itself, now to appear in the presence of God for us."*
> *— Hebrews 9:24*

When Yeshua ascended into heaven, He did not disappear into mystery—He entered into ministry. He did not cease being our Priest; He began the fullness of that role. Everything the earthly tabernacle foreshadowed now finds its perfect fulfillment—not in Jerusalem's temple of stone, but in the heavenly sanctuary above.

This is the blazing center of the gospel:

We have a Priest who lives.

We have a Priest who ministers.

We have a Priest who stands before the Father—for us.

The Earthly Shadow

The tabernacle in the wilderness—given to Moses—was patterned after something real: the heavenly sanctuary. As Hebrews 8:5 declares:

> *"[The priests] serve unto the example and shadow of heavenly things, as Moses was admonished ...See that thou make all things according to the pattern shewed to thee in the mount.'"*

The veil, the altar, the mercy seat—all these were copies. They pointed to a heavenly reality that only Yeshua could enter, and that only His blood could cleanse.

The Levitical priests stood in the copy.

Yeshua stands in the original.

The Veil Torn on Earth, the Way Opened in Heaven

When Jesus died, "the veil of the temple was rent in twain from the top to the bottom" (*Matthew 27:51*). This was not a symbolic gesture. It was a divine declaration:

> The way into the Holy of Holies was now open—not on earth, but in heaven.

Hebrews 10:19–20:

> *"Having therefore, brethren, boldness to enter into the holiest by the blood of Jesus, by a new and living way... through the veil, that is to say, his flesh..."*

The body of Christ is the veil that was torn. And through Him, we now have access—not to a copy—but to the throne of God.

The Heavenly Office of the Son

In Hebrews 9:24, we are told something that should stun the soul:

> *"Christ is... entered into heaven itself, now to appear in the presence of God for us."*

The Greek word used—emphanisthēnai—means to present oneself in an official capacity, as an advocate or representative. Jesus, having offered His own blood, now stands in the court of the Almighty on your behalf.

He is not waiting to begin His priesthood.

He is functioning in it—now.

He is actively mediating the covenant. He is receiving your prayers. He is applying the power of His once-for-all sacrifice to the life of every believer.

The Golden Altar of Intercession

Revelation 8:3–4 shows us the heavenly altar:

> *"And another angel came and stood at the altar, having a golden censer; and there was given unto him much incense, that he should offer it with the prayers of all saints..."*

Our Great High Priest stands before that altar—not with incense only, but with intercession.

He is the fulfillment of the golden censer, the High Priest's garments, the Ark, and the blood upon the mercy seat.

There is not a corner of heaven's temple where His presence is not known.

The Greater and More Perfect Tabernacle

Hebrews 9:11:

> *"But Christ being come an high priest of good things to come, by a greater and more perfect tabernacle, not made with hands..."*

Every earthly priest stood on shifting sand. Their ministry was limited by location, by sin, and by death.

But Jesus entered a sanctuary not made with hands—eternal, perfect, incorruptible.

No dust can enter it. No decay. No death.

And there, He remains—not repeating the sacrifice, but applying its power forever.

The Blood That Speaks

Hebrews 12:24 says:

> *"And to Jesus the mediator of the new covenant, and to the blood of sprinkling, that speaketh better things than that of Abel."*

In the heavenly sanctuary, there is blood.

But it is not the blood of bulls or goats.

It is not a reminder of wrath.

It is the blood of Yeshua—and it speaks of mercy, forgiveness, cleansing, adoption, and victory.

It does not fade. It does not spoil. It has no expiration date.

And it is heard in heaven, every moment, over every child of God.

The Living Way

There is a living way now opened. We do not approach God by ritual, religion, or race.

We approach Him by:
- A High Priest who passed through the heavens (Hebrews 4:14)
- A Lamb whose blood is eternally fresh
- A throne of grace, not of condemnation
- A sanctuary that will never be defiled

The invitation is not to come in fear, but in faith.

Hebrews 4:16:

> *"Let us therefore come boldly unto the throne of grace, that we may obtain mercy, and find grace to help in time of need."*

Ministry in the Age to Come

Christ's priesthood is not bound by time.

He is the same yesterday, today, and forever.

And even in the New Heavens and New Earth, the Lamb will still be the Light. The Throne will still be the center. And worship will flow from the eternal ministry of the King-Priest.

Revelation 7:17 says:

> *"For the Lamb which is in the midst of the throne shall feed them, and shall lead them unto living fountains of waters..."*

He will never cease being our Priest.

Your Anchor Within the Veil
Hebrews 6:19-20:

> *"Which hope we have as an anchor of the soul, both sure and steadfast, and which entereth into that within the veil; Whither the forerunner is for us entered, even Jesus..."*

Your hope is not in a doctrine.

Your anchor is not in a building.

It is in a person—Jesus, the Forerunner, who entered within the veil, and who holds you there by His intercession, blood, and love.

He has not forgotten you.

He has not abandoned you.

He is at work, right now, in the sanctuary of the heavens—for you.

A Royal Priesthood — How Believers Share in the Order

> *"But ye are a chosen generation, a royal priesthood, an holy nation, a peculiar people..."* — 1 Peter 2:9

Most believers know that Christ is our High Priest.

Fewer realize that we have been called to be priests, too.

Not in the old Levitical sense—sacrificing animals, standing behind altars—but in the heavenly order of Melchizedek, the order of the risen Christ. The priesthood of Jesus was not meant to end with Him—it was meant to include us.

This is not theory. It is not a metaphor. It is your identity.

You are not just redeemed. You are ordained.

The Priesthood Restored to the People

When God first called Israel out of Egypt, His desire was clear:

> *"Ye shall be unto me a kingdom of priests, and an holy nation."*
> *— Exodus 19:6*

But after the sin of the golden calf, only the tribe of Levi was chosen to serve in the tabernacle (*Exodus 32:26–29*). The nation forfeited what was originally meant for all.

Yet in Christ, the veil has been torn. The restrictions have been removed. The priesthood is restored—and not just to a tribe, but to a people born again by the Spirit.

From Shadows to Substance

In the old covenant:

- Priests were born into the right family.
- They wore garments set apart.
- They offered sacrifices daily.
- Their ministry was limited by time, sin, and death.

But now, in the new covenant:

- We are born from above (*John 3:3*) into a spiritual lineage.
- We are clothed with robes of righteousness (*Isaiah 61:10*).
- We offer spiritual sacrifices (*1 Peter 2:5*).
- Our service is empowered by the eternal Spirit (*Hebrews 9:14*).

This is not less real than the Levitical system. It is more real—because it is eternal.

Priests After the Order of Christ

Jesus is not just our representative. He is our prototype.

He is the firstborn among many brethren (*Romans 8:29*).

He was not only anointed—He anoints us.

1 John 2:27:

> "*But the anointing which ye have received of him abideth in you...*"

We share in His priesthood because we share in His life.

And His life is that of a King-Priest.

What Does a Royal Priest Do?

1. Offers Spiritual Sacrifices

"Ye also... are built up a spiritual house, an holy priesthood, to offer up spiritual sacrifices, acceptable to God by Jesus Christ."
— *1 Peter 2:5*

What are these sacrifices?

- Praise: "The fruit of our lips giving thanks to His name"
  (Hebrews 13:15)
- Prayer: "The incense of the saints"
  (Revelation 5:8)
- Obedience: "To do good and to communicate forget not"
  (Hebrews 13:16)
- Our bodies: "A living sacrifice, holy, acceptable unto God..."
  (Romans 12:1)

Your daily devotion is your priestly duty.

2. Stands in Intercession

Like the priests of old, we stand between heaven and earth—interceding, weeping, pleading, and declaring God's will.

Ezekiel 22:30:

"I sought for a man among them, that should make up the hedge, and stand in the gap..."

Every believer is called to stand in the gap—for family, for nations, for the lost.

3. Ministers to the Presence of God

Priests don't just serve people—they minister to God Himself.

Ezekiel 44:15:

"They shall come near to me to minister unto me, and they shall stand before me..."

When you worship in secret...

When you wait in His presence...

When you offer tears and trust—

You are performing priestly service before the throne.

Clothed in Righteousness
Revelation 1:6:
> *"[Jesus] hath made us kings and priests unto God and his Father..."*

This is not a poetic flourish. It is a heavenly reality. The blood of Jesus has not only washed us—it has invested us with garments of holiness, authority, and access.

Isaiah 61:10:
> *"He hath clothed me with the garments of salvation, he hath covered me with the robe of righteousness..."*

You do not serve in your own strength.
You serve clothed in Christ.

The Royal Crown and the Golden Censer
In Zechariah 6:13, a prophecy is spoken:
> *"...He shall be a priest upon his throne..."*

This was unthinkable in Israel. A king could not be a priest. But in Yeshua, the two offices are joined. And we, united to Him, carry both authority and intimacy, both dominion and devotion.

You are not just called to rule. You are called to minister.
You are not just redeemed to escape hell. You are redeemed to approach heaven.

A Kingdom of Priests
Revelation 5:10:
> *"[Thou] hast made us unto our God kings and priests: and we shall reign on the earth."*

This is the destiny of the believer. Not only to worship in heaven—but to reign with Christ on earth.

- Priests minister in the secret place.
- Kings govern in the public square.
- In Christ, we are called to both.

You are not irrelevant in this age.

You are not insignificant in God's kingdom.

You are anointed, appointed, and sent.

Living as a Royal Priest Today

To walk in this priesthood is to embrace:

- Access: You may come boldly to the throne (*Hebrews 4:16*)
- Responsibility: You are called to minister in prayer, worship, and Word
- Authority: You reign with Christ now, in spirit, and in the age to come

You are not a spectator in the gospel. You are a priest in the drama of redemption.

Your prayers matter. Your praise shifts atmospheres. Your intercession touches heaven.

Chapter IX
The End of the Old, The Reign of the Eternal

How the Melchizedek Priesthood Transforms Our Worship, Identity, and Access to God

The curtain has been torn.

The altar has been moved.

The sacrifice has been offered once and for all.

The priesthood has changed—and with it, everything has shifted.

For generations, the people of God approached Him through a system of types and shadows—temples made by hands, priests from the tribe of Levi, sacrifices that had to be repeated daily, yearly, endlessly. The blood of bulls and goats flowed as a symbol, but it could never truly cleanse the conscience (*Hebrews 10:1–4*). This old order, glorious in its time, has now been eclipsed by a glory that will never fade—the priesthood after the order of Melchizedek, fulfilled eternally in Yeshua the Messiah.

The Old Fades Away

The writer of Hebrews declared with bold clarity:

> *"For the priesthood being changed, there is made of necessity a change also of the law." — Hebrews 7:12*

This is no small transition. The Mosaic priesthood was built upon lineage, regulation, and ritual. Access to God was limited, veiled, and distant. Only the high priest could enter the Most Holy Place, and that only once a year, and never without blood. It was a system that held the people of God at arm's length—merciful, but not intimate. Necessary, but not permanent. When Yeshua came, He did not arise from the tribe of Levi. He came from Judah—a tribe without priestly association—yet He was declared a priest forever by oath, not by bloodline. His priesthood was not based on the flesh, but on "the power of an endless life" (*Hebrews 7:16*). In that very shift, the old system was made obsolete:

> *"In that he saith, A new covenant, he hath made the first old. Now that which decayeth and waxeth old is ready to vanish away."*
> *— Hebrews 8:13*

The shadows were passing. The reality had come.

The Living Priest and Open Access

Unlike the Levitical priests who served until death interrupted their ministry, Yeshua lives forever. He holds His priesthood unchangeably. He doesn't retire. He doesn't need successors. He intercedes continually—not from earth, but from heaven itself. He ministers not in the temple made with hands, but in the heavenly sanctuary, before the throne of the Father (*Hebrews 9:24*).

The implications of this are staggering.

Access to God is no longer limited. The veil has been torn from top to bottom (*Matthew 27:51*). Worship is no longer confined to temples, garments, or annual festivals. It is now spirit and truth—heart to heart, face to face. The High Priest is no longer in a back room behind a curtain. He is seated on the mercy seat of heaven—and He calls us to draw near:

> *"Let us therefore come boldly unto the throne of grace, that we may obtain mercy, and find grace to help in time of need."*
> — *Hebrews 4:16*

This is not mere theology. This is transformation.

Worship Transformed

The priesthood of Melchizedek redefines worship. It is no longer about ritual performance. It is about relational proximity. Worship is no longer a duty—it is a response. We worship not to gain access to God, but because we already have it. The blood has spoken. The way has been opened. In this new order, worship is led not by Levitical songbooks but by the Spirit of God Himself. The believer becomes both temple and priest—indwelt by the Spirit, offering spiritual sacrifices acceptable to God through Yeshua the Messiah (*1 Peter 2:5*).

Identity Transformed

In Messiah, we are not spectators—we are priests.

> *"But ye are a chosen generation, a royal priesthood, an holy nation, a peculiar people..."*
> — *1 Peter 2:9*

The priesthood of Melchizedek is not an exclusive club. It is a royal calling extended to all who are in Christ. We are robed in righteousness, crowned with mercy, and commissioned to offer intercession, thanksgiving, praise, and witness. Our identity is no longer defined by tribe or genealogy—it is anchored in the blood of the Lamb and the power of His resurrection. The believer becomes both sanctuary and servant. We do not approach God through others—we approach through Christ, and we become ministers in His name.

Access Transformed

Perhaps the most revolutionary truth of this new priesthood is this: you are welcome. Not tolerated—welcomed. Not barely accepted—adopted.

The Melchizedek priesthood tears down every dividing wall. Jew and Gentile, man and woman, servant and free—no one is barred. There is now one High Priest, one Mediator, one Lamb—and all who come through Him are received without hesitation.

No more fear. No more trembling at Sinai. We have come to Mount Zion, to the city of the Living God (*Hebrews 12:22–24*). We worship under an open heaven.

The Eternal Reign

This priesthood is not temporary. It does not waver with empires or eras. It is anchored in eternity. Yeshua is not only the Great High Priest—He is the King of Glory. The priest is seated on the throne. The order of Melchizedek is royal and righteous. It governs now and forever.

Every act of prayer, every word of praise, every tear in intercession passes through this eternal priesthood. It is sanctified by the blood of Christ, and empowered by the Spirit of God.

This is the reign of the eternal—the end of the old, and the beginning of everlasting access.

> *"By so much was Jesus made a surety of a better testament."*
> *— Hebrews 7:22*

The order has changed. The veil is gone.

Let the redeemed rise and minister.

Let every believer take their place in the priesthood of the Lamb—

who lives forever, who reigns forever, who intercedes forever.

The fire of Melchizedek still burns.

And we now serve in its flame.

Conclusion

The Fire Still Burns — Our Priest, Our Access, Our Call

The veil was torn, but the fire never died.

From the shadowed valley where Melchizedek stepped into the story with bread and wine…

To the blood-soaked hill outside Jerusalem where the eternal High Priest offered Himself once and for all…

To the throne room of heaven where He now intercedes with eyes like fire and a crown that does not fade…

The priesthood has never been silenced. It has only been fulfilled.

What began as a mystery in Genesis, spoken again in Psalms, and thundered forth in Hebrews, now resounds in the heart of every believer.

This is not ancient theology—it is present reality. The order of Melchizedek is not a lost relic—it is the eternal order that governs the heavens and calls forth the Church.

He was without beginning, and He shall have no end.

Yeshua, the King of Righteousness.

Yeshua, the Prince of Peace.

Yeshua, the Priest forever—not by the law of a carnal commandment, but by the power of an endless life.

He is not behind a curtain. He is not seated in silence. He reigns.

And He is calling us to draw near.

What Now?

The old priesthood was about distance.

This one is about access.

The old priesthood required repetition.

This one declares, "It is finished."

The old priesthood served on earth.

This one ministers in heaven.

The old priesthood waited for the next generation.

This one endures forever.

So what does that mean for us?

It means you are not merely a believer—you are a priest.

It means your worship is not noise—it is incense.

It means your intercession is not wishful thinking—it is royal protocol.

It means you stand in the fire that never goes out.

You are a royal priesthood. A holy nation. A people purchased by blood.

You no longer approach the throne trembling. You approach it boldly—because your High Priest lives.

The order of Melchizedek is not just a mystery solved. It is a movement continued.

So come.

Come to the table where the Bread and Wine are eternal.

Come to the throne where mercy never runs dry.

Come to the sanctuary not built with hands, where the Lamb is the Light.

Come not as a stranger—but as a priest in the order of the One who reigns.

Let your worship rise like smoke.

Let your prayers pierce the heavens.

Let your life be a holy offering on the altar that cannot be shaken.

For the Priest still reigns.

And His kingdom shall have no end.

Glossary of Terms

Covenant — A sacred and binding agreement between God and man. The New Covenant, established by Christ, supersedes the Mosaic Covenant and grants access to God through grace.

Hebrews 5–7 — A critical New Testament passage unpacking how Yeshua fulfills and surpasses the Levitical priesthood by entering into the eternal priesthood of Melchizedek.

Intercession — The act of standing in the gap on behalf of another. Yeshua, our High Priest, ever lives to make intercession for us.

Levitical Priesthood — The priesthood descending from the tribe of Levi, specifically through Aaron. It was established under the Mosaic Covenant and governed temple sacrifices and rituals.

Melchizedek (מַלְכִּי־צֶדֶק) — A mysterious priest-king of Salem who appears in Genesis 14, offering bread and wine to Abraham. His name means "King of Righteousness," and he is also called "King of Salem," meaning "King of Peace." He serves as a divine foreshadowing of Christ.

Messiah (מָשִׁיחַ/ Christ) — The Anointed One. Yeshua (Jesus) is the promised deliverer and eternal High Priest, fulfilling the shadow and substance of Melchizedek.

Order of Melchizedek — A divine priesthood not based on genealogy, law, or time. It is eternal, heavenly, and fulfilled in the person and priesthood of Christ.

Priesthood — The office or function of a priest. In biblical terms, it represents one who is appointed by God to stand in the gap between God and man through intercession, offering, and blessing.

Psalm 110 — A prophetic psalm declaring the eternal priesthood of the Messiah "after the order of Melchizedek." It is the most quoted Old Testament chapter in the New Testament.

Royal Priesthood — The collective identity of believers in Christ who are both kings and priests, called to minister, reign, and intercede under His authority.

Salem — An early name for Jerusalem. The place over which Melchizedek was king.

Sanctuary — The holy place of God's presence. In the Old Covenant, it was the Tabernacle or Temple. In the New Covenant, it is the heavenly realm where Yeshua ministers on our behalf.

Throne of Grace — The heavenly seat of divine authority and mercy where believers now have direct access through the blood of Christ.

Tithe — A tenth portion, often of one's income or possessions, given as an act of worship. Abraham gave a tithe to Melchizedek as a sign of honor and submission.

Veil — The curtain in the Tabernacle/Temple that separated the Holy of Holies. Torn at the death of Jesus, symbolizing open access to God through the Eternal High Priest.

Scripture Index

Genesis
- Genesis 14:18–20 — Melchizedek blesses Abram and offers bread and wine
- Genesis 12:1–3 — The call and blessing of Abram
- Genesis 15:6 — Abram believed the Lord
- Genesis 22:17–18 — Blessing through Abraham's seed

Exodus
- Exodus 28:1 — The establishment of the Levitical priesthood
- Exodus 33:11 — The Lord spoke to Moses face to face

Leviticus
- Leviticus 16 — The Day of Atonement
- Leviticus 21:17–23 — Priestly qualifications

Numbers
- Numbers 18:21 — Tithes given to the Levites

Deuteronomy
- Deuteronomy 10:8 — Priestly service and intercession

2 Samuel
- 2 Samuel 7:12–13 — Davidic covenant

Psalm
- Psalm 110:1–4 — "Thou art a priest forever after the order of Melchizedek"

- Psalm 2:6–9 — The enthronement of the Son
- Psalm 24 — The King of Glory

Isaiah

- Isaiah 9:6–7 — A child is born… Prince of Peace
- Isaiah 53 — The suffering servant

Jeremiah

- Jeremiah 31:31–34 — The New Covenant

Zechariah

- Zechariah 6:13 — The priest on the throne

Matthew

- Matthew 27:51 — The veil of the temple was torn

Luke

- Luke 24:27 — Beginning at Moses and all the prophets

John

- John 1:1 — In the beginning was the Word
- John 1:29 — Behold the Lamb of God
- John 14:6 — I am the way, the truth, and the life

Acts

- Acts 7:1–53 — Stephen's retelling of the Abrahamic and priestly story

Romans

- Romans 4:3 — Abraham believed God
- Romans 8:34 — Christ intercedes for us

1 Corinthians

- 1 Corinthians 11:23–26 — Bread and wine in the Lord's Supper

2 Corinthians

- 2 Corinthians 3:6 — Ministers of the New Covenant

Galatians
- Galatians 3:6–9 — Those of faith are sons of Abraham
- Galatians 4:4–7 — Fullness of time, adoption

Ephesians
- Ephesians 2:18 — Access to the Father
- Ephesians 4:11–13 — The priestly ministry of the Church

Philippians
- Philippians 2:9–11 — Every knee shall bow

Hebrews
- Hebrews 1:3 — He sat down at the right hand
- Hebrews 4:14–16 — Our great High Priest
- Hebrews 5:1–10 — Christ called after the order of Melchizedek
- Hebrews 6:19–20 — Hope as an anchor; Jesus our forerunner
- Hebrews 7 — The full teaching on Melchizedek
- Hebrews 8:1–6 — The heavenly sanctuary
- Hebrews 9:11–15 — The blood of Christ in the heavenly tabernacle
- Hebrews 10:19–22 — Boldness to enter the Most Holy Place

1 Peter
- 1 Peter 2:9 — A royal priesthood

Revelation
- Revelation 1:5–6 — Made us kings and priests
- Revelation 5:9–10 — Priests to reign on the earth
- Revelation 21:22 — No temple; the Lord God Almighty is the temple

Bibliography & References

For The Order of Melchizedek: The Eternal Priesthood of Christ Revealed By Damiano B. Centola

Primary Scriptural Sources
- The Holy Bible, King James Version (KJV)
- The Holy Scriptures, English Standard Version (ESV)
- Biblia Hebraica Stuttgartensia — Edited by K. Elliger and W. Rudolph
- Septuaginta — Rahlfs-Hanhart Edition
- The Greek New Testament, UBS 5th Edition
- The Dead Sea Scrolls — Translations and Commentary, ed. Geza Vermes
- Targum Onkelos and Targum Jonathan — English Translations

Key Biblical Passages Cited
- Genesis 14:17–24 — Appearance of Melchizedek
- Psalm 110 — Eternal priesthood declared
- Hebrews 5–7 — Christ as High Priest in the order of Melchizedek
- 1 Peter 2:9 — The royal priesthood of believers
- Exodus 28–29; Leviticus 8–10 — Priestly ordination and duties
- Matthew 27:50–51 — The veil torn
- Revelation 1:6; 5:10 — Reign of priests and kings with Christ

Scholarly and Theological Works

Bruce, F. F. The Epistle to the Hebrews. New International Commentary on the New Testament. Eerdmans, 1990.

- Kaiser, Walter C. The Messiah in the Old Testament. Zondervan, 1995.
- Owen, John. An Exposition of the Epistle to the Hebrews. Banner of Truth Trust (Reprint), 1991.
- Lane, William L. Hebrews 1–8 & Hebrews 9–13. Word Biblical Commentary. Thomas Nelson, 1991.
- Wright, N. T. Jesus and the Victory of God. Fortress Press, 1996.
- Keener, Craig S. The IVP Bible Background Commentary: New Testament. InterVarsity Press, 1993.
- Hamilton, Victor P. The Book of Genesis: Chapters 1–17. NICOT, Eerdmans, 1990.
- Wenham, Gordon J. Genesis 1–15. Word Biblical Commentary. Thomas Nelson, 1987.
- Delitzsch, Franz. Biblical Commentary on the Psalms. T&T Clark, 1871.
- Rashi. Commentary on the Torah — Translated by Artscroll, Mesorah Publications
- Josephus. Antiquities of the Jews. Trans. William Whiston

Jewish and Rabbinic Sources

- Mishnah Torah — Maimonides, ed. Philip Birnbaum
- Talmud Bavli, Tractates Berakhot, Sanhedrin, and Yoma
- Midrash Rabbah on Genesis and Psalms
- Zohar (for historical comparison; not doctrinal authority)

Messianic & Theological Reflections

- Fruchtenbaum, Arnold G. Messianic Christology. Ariel Ministries, 1998.
- David H. Stern, Jewish New Testament Commentary. Jewish New Testament Publications, 1992.
- Pink, Arthur W. The Priesthood of Christ. Moody Publishers, 1937.
- Spurgeon, Charles H. The Treasury of David. Hendrickson Publishers, 1988 (reprint)
- Bonhoeffer, Dietrich. Christ the Center. HarperOne, 1978.

Acknowledgments

To the Eternal High Priest, Yeshua the Messiah — this book is for You. You are the fulfillment of every mystery, the fire behind every altar, and the reason the veil was torn.

To my beloved wife, Feebe, your unwavering faith, prophetic wisdom, and quiet strength are the sanctuary where this revelation was nurtured. You have been the steady rhythm beneath my words and the living song behind my worship. Thank you for walking beside me in both the fire and the glory.

To my father, Pop, a man of vision and holy conviction. You have seen the Lord, and your life speaks volumes more than ink ever could. Your voice echoes through these pages, and your legacy will never fade.

To the remnant—those who have not bowed to the spirit of this age. You know who you are. Your hunger for truth, your prayers in the night, your fire on the altar have inspired me to write with precision and boldness.

To the scholars, theologians, and scribes who have preserved the Scriptures with care, and to the early Church fathers and martyrs who bled so that this truth could reach our generation—I honor you.

To every pastor, teacher, and intercessor who understands the weight of the priestly calling—not just in title but in tears—thank you for bearing the flame.

To Paula Garcia and the entire team at Explorabooks, your creative excellence and unwavering support have made this vision soar. You believed in the prophetic potential of this project before the ink dried.

And finally, to the readers. May this book ignite something eternal in you. You were not just made to survive this world. You were chosen to minister before the throne of God in the order of a Priest who lives forever. Never forget who you are.

With gratitude, awe, and reverence,

—Damiano B. Centola

About the Author

Damiano B. Centola is a visionary theologian, spiritual architect, and author of over twenty groundbreaking works that bridge the ancient world and eternal truth. With a passion for Scripture and sacred design, his works blend biblical scholarship with prophetic insight, uncovering deep mysteries often hidden in plain sight.

Damiano's research has reshaped how we understand divine patterns—from The Mystery of Mysteries: Decoding the Divine Proportions of the Human Body Through Art, Anatomy, and Sacred Geometry to Bloodline: The Battle for Divine DNA. He writes with the precision of a scholar, the passion of a poet, and the humility of a servant.

He lives in Los Angeles with his wife Feebe Huang, where he continues to write, teach, and create Spirit-led works that awaken hearts across the globe.

Back Cover Blurb

"Before Aaron, before Levi—there was Melchizedek."

Who was this mysterious priest-king who appeared to Abraham with bread and wine? Why does Scripture declare him a priest forever? And what does his ancient priesthood mean for believers today?

In The Order of Melchizedek: The Eternal Priesthood of Christ Revealed, acclaimed author and theologian Damiano B. Centola unearths one of the most profound mysteries in the Bible—one that stretches from the valley of Salem to the throne room of heaven. This deeply theological and spiritually stirring book unveils:

- The identity and function of Melchizedek in Genesis
- Why his priesthood supersedes Levi's
- How Psalm 110 and Hebrews build the case for a better covenant
- The role of Yeshua (Jesus) as both Priest and King in the heavenly sanctuary
- How believers today are called into this royal priesthood

From ancient encounters to eternal truths, this book explores the awe-inspiring beauty of Christ's priestly reign—a priesthood not inherited by bloodline, but ordained by God Himself.

Prepare to be transformed.

This is not just a study of history—it's a revelation of your identity, your worship, and your divine access to the Father.

www.ingramcontent.com/pod-product-compliance
Lightning Source LLC
Chambersburg PA
CBHW061224070526
44584CB00029B/3973